Secrets of SEO: techniques for climbing Google rankings

by

Gubitosa Pierfranco

Preface

In the digital age in which we live, the success of an online business no longer depends solely on the quality of the product or service offered. At the heart of a winning digital marketing strategy is the ability to be found by one's potential customers at the exact moment they search for information, solutions or products on the Internet. This is where search engine optimization, better known as SEO (Search Engine Optimization), comes in.

"The Secrets of SEO: Sound Techniques for Climbing Google Rankings" was created with the goal of guiding you through the complex dynamics of search engine optimization. Whether you are a business owner eager to increase the visibility of your online business, a marketer intent on perfecting your skills or simply a digital enthusiast, this book is designed to provide you with practical tools and effective strategies.

SEO is an ever-evolving discipline, influenced by Google's frequent algorithm updates and changing user search habits. In this context, staying up-to-date on best practices is crucial. Our intent is to make concepts that can often seem complex accessible and understandable by providing clear and detailed guidance that can be followed step by step.

The book is structured to cover every fundamental aspect of SEO: from keyword analysis to quality content creation, from technical site optimization to building a strong link network. Each chapter is enriched with concrete cxamples, case studies, and practical tips from years of experience and experimentation in the field.

But SEO is not just about technique. At the heart of any winning strategy is a deep understanding of your audience's needs and the ability to deliver real value through content. Therefore, special attention is paid to the importance of creating a positive user experience and content that truly responds to visitors' questions and needs.

By reading "The Secrets of SEO," you will learn not only the most effective techniques for improving your site's ranking on Google, but also how to develop a mindset of continuous improvement and adaptation. In a digital landscape where competition is increasingly fierce, the ability to evolve and adopt best practices will make the difference between success and anonymity.

With the hope that this book will be a valuable resource in your journey, we invite you to dive into reading it with curiosity and determination. Climbing the Google rankings is an exciting challenge, and we are here to accompany you step by step.

Happy reading and enjoy your work!

Pierfranco Gubitosa

Index

6. **Use of Social Media**

- The influence of social media on SEO
- Content sharing strategies
- Building an online community
- Monitoring social media engagement

7. **User Experience (UX)**

- Importance of UX for SEO
- Intuitive design and easy navigation
- Optimization for loading speed
- Continuous testing and improvement of the UX

8. **Local SEO**

- Understanding local SEO
- Google My Business Optimization
- Collection and management of reviews
- Strategies for local activities

9. **Monitoring and Analysis**

- SEO analysis tools
- Monitoring traffic and site performance
- Keyword and content analysis
- Using Google Analytics and Google Search Console

10.   **SEO for E-commerce**

- Specificity of SEO for e-commerce sites
- Optimization of product sheets
- SEO for product categories
- Strategies to increase conversion rate

11.   **Multimedia Content**

INTRODUCTION TO SEO

What is SEO?

SEO (Search Engine Optimization) is the set of techniques and strategies used to improve the visibility of a website in the organic results of search engines, mainly Google. The main goal of SEO is to increase organic traffic to the site by improving its ranking in SERPs (Search Engine Results Pages). SEO is divided into two macro areas:

1. **On-Page SEO**: It concerns the optimization of internal website elements, such as content, meta descriptions, H1, H2 tags, images, site structure and page loading speed.
2. **Off-Page SEO**: These are all those activities outside the website such as backlink building, social media marketing, online mentions and other techniques to improve the site's authority and relevance in the eyes of search engines.

The importance of SEO in digital marketing

SEO is a key element of digital marketing for several reasons but the main ones can be summarized in four and they are:

1. **Visibility and Organic Traffic**: A good ranking in search results increases the visibility of the website, leading to an increase in organic traffic. The higher the ranking, the more likely it is that users will visit the site.

2. **Credibility and Trust**: Users tend to trust Google's organic results more than paid ads. Being

ranked among the top results suggests to users that the site is authoritative and relevant and worth visiting.

3. **Cost-Effectiveness**: Compared to paid advertising campaigns (such as Google Ads), SEO can be more cost-effective de cheap in the long run. Once the site is well positioned, organic traffic continues to flow without significant additional expense.

4. **User Experience**: SEO is not only about search engines but also about user experience. An optimized site is often faster, mobile-friendly and easier to navigate, improving user satisfaction.

Evolution of Google's algorithms

Google's algorithms are constantly evolving to improve the quality of search results and combat spam. Here are some of the major evolutionary milestones:

1. **Google Panda (2011)**: Introduced to penalize sites with low quality and duplicate content. Encouraged the creation of original, high-quality content.

2. **Google Penguin (2012)**: It hit sites that used manipulative link-building techniques. It pushed toward more natural and authentic backlink building.

3. **Hummingbird (2013)**: Improved understanding of search queries by introducing the concept of semantic search. Google has become better at understanding the context and intent behind user queries.

4. **RankBrain (2015)**: An artificial intelligence system that helps Google better interpret search queries and deliver more relevant results. It is particularly effective at processing complex, never-before-seen queries.

5. **BERT (2019)**: A further evolution of semantic search, BERT helps Google better understand the nuances and context of words in search queries.

Realistic goals and expectations

When starting an SEO strategy, it is important to have clear goals and realistic expectations. Here are some key points to follow to the letter to make sure you get results:

1. **Time and Patience**: SEO is a long-term strategy. Significant results can take months, sometimes even a year. It is important not to expect immediate improvements.

2. **Analysis and Monitoring**: Use tools such as Google Analytics and Google Search Console to monitor site performance and adjust SEO strategy based on the data collected.

3. **Quality Content**: Creating high-quality, relevant and useful content for target audiences is critical. Google's algorithms reward sites that provide value to users.

4. **Natural Link-Building**: Avoid manipulative link-building techniques. Focus on building genuine relationships and getting backlinks from authoritative and relevant sites.

5. **Constant Adaptation**: Search engine algorithms are constantly evolving. It is essential to stay current on the latest SEO trends and best practices to maintain and improve rankings.

In conclusion, SEO is a crucial element of digital marketing that requires a strategic and patient approach. With the right combination of on-page and off-page techniques, constant analysis and a focus on quality content, it is possible to achieve significant results in the long term.

KEYWORD RESEARCH

Keyword research is a key component of SEO. Identifying the right keywords allows you to drive traffic to your website in an effective and targeted manner. In this chapter we explain how to understand search intent, the tools available for keyword research, the difference between long-tail and short-tail keywords, and how to analyze your competition.

Understand the research intent

Understanding search intent means understanding what users are actually looking for when they type a particular keyword into a search engine. Search intent generally falls into three main categories:

1. **Informational Intention**: Users are looking for information on a specific topic. Examples of keywords include "how to bake bread" or "what is SEO."

2. **Navigational Intent**: Users search for a specific website. Examples of keywords include "Facebook login" or "official Apple site."

3. **Transactional Intention**: Users have the intention to make a purchase or take a specific action. Examples of keywords include "buy shoes online" or "subscribe to Netflix."

Keyword research tools

There are several tools that help with keyword research, each with unique features:

1. **Google Keyword Planner**: A free tool offered by Google Ads that provides data on keyword search volume and related suggestions.
2. **SEMrush**: A comprehensive SEO suite offering keyword, competitive, and website analysis.
3. **Ahrefs**: Known for its robust backlink database, Ahrefs also provides tools for keyword research and competitive analysis.
4. **Moz Keyword Explorer**: Another powerful tool for finding relevant keywords and analyzing ranking difficulty.
5. **Ubersuggest**: Created by Neil Patel, it is a free tool that offers keyword suggestions and search volume analysis.

Long-tail keywords vs. short-tail keywords

Keywords can be divided into two main categories: long-tail keywords and direct keywords.

1. **Direct keywords**: These are generic search terms consisting of one or two words. Examples include "shoes," "SEO," or "digital marketing." These keywords tend to have a high search volume, but they are also highly competitive and less specific.

2. **Long-tail keywords**: These are more specific phrases consisting of three or more words.

Examples include "running shoes for women," "SEO strategies for e-commerce," or "how to do digital marketing for small businesses." These keywords tend to have lower search volume but are less competitive and more targeted. Users using long-tail keywords often have a clearer and more specific search intention, which can lead to higher conversion rates.

Competitive analysis

Competitor analysis is an important step in keyword research. It allows you to identify what keywords competitors are using and how they are ranking for these words. Here are some steps for conducting an effective analysis:

1. **Identify Competitors**: Identify the main competitors in your industry. You can do this by simply searching for the major keywords in your industry and observing which sites appear on the first pages of Web search engines.

2. **Use Analysis Tools**: Tools such as SEMrush, Ahrefs and Moz can help you analyze the keywords your competitors are ranking for. These tools provide information on search volume, ranking difficulty and backlinks of competitor sites.

3. **Analyze Competitor Content**: Examine the content of competitor sites that rank well for keywords of interest. Pay attention to content

quality, structure, keywords used, and link-building strategies.

4. **Identify Opportunities**: After analyzing the competition, try to identify gaps and opportunities. Are there relevant keywords for your industry that competitors are not exploiting? Are there areas where you can create better, more detailed content?

To recapitulate.

Keyword research is essential to an effective SEO strategy. Understanding search intent, using the right tools, choosing between long-tail and short-tail keywords, and analyzing your competition are all key steps to direct traffic to your site in a targeted and optimal way. With thorough and well-planned keyword research, you can significantly improve your search engine rankings and achieve your digital marketing goals.

ON PAGE OPTIMIZATION

On-page optimization is a part of SEO that focuses on improving individual elements of a website to rank higher in search results and attract relevant traffic. In this chapter I explain quality content creation, the importance of meta tags, URL structure, and the effective use of keywords in content.

Quality content creation

Content is at the heart of on-page SEO. Google and other search engines reward sites that offer high-quality content that is relevant and useful to users. Here are some tips for creating quality content:

1. **Originality and uniqueness**: Avoid duplicate content. Each page should offer unique and original information.
2. **Relevance**: Make sure your content is relevant to users' search queries. Understand your audience and answer their questions.
3. **Insight**: Provide detailed and in-depth content. Long, well-structured and informative pages tend to rank better.
4. **Readability**: Use clear and simple language. Structure the text with short paragraphs, bulleted lists and headings to facilitate reading.
5. **Regular update**: Keep content updated to respond to changes and new information.

Meta tags: Titles and descriptions

Meta tags are HTML elements that provide information to search engines and users about the contents of a page. The most important are the meta title and meta description.

1. **Meta title**: This is the title that appears in search results. It should be clear, concise and contain the main keyword of the page. The ideal length is between 50 and 60 characters.

   - **Sample**: "Complete Guide to SEO: Strategies and Tips for 2024"

2. **Meta description**: This is a brief description of the page content that appears below the title in search results. It should be persuasive and contain the main keyword. The ideal length is between 150 and 160 characters.

   - **Example**: "Learn how to improve your website ranking with our comprehensive guide to SEO. Updated Strategies for 2024."

Structure of URLs

URL structure is an often overlooked but important element for on-page optimization. A well-structured URL is easy for users and search engines to read. Here are some best practices:

1. **Simplicity**: URLs should be simple and easy to read. Avoid numbers and special characters.

2. **Keywords**: Include the main keyword in the URL to improve relevance.

3. **Separation**: Use hyphens to separate words in the URL. Avoid the use of underscores and other symbols.

4. **Length**: Keep URLs short and descriptive. Avoid long and complex URLs.

   - **Example**: "https://www.esempio.com/guida-seo-2024"

Effective use of keywords in content

Effective use of keywords is essential for on-page optimization. However, it is important to use keywords naturally and not in a forced way. Here are some tips:

1. **Natural insertion**: Keywords should be integrated naturally into the text. Avoid keyword stuffing, which can be penalizing.
2. **Titles and subtitles**: Use main keywords in titles (H1, H2, H3) to improve relevance and readability.
3. **First paragraphs**: Include keywords in the first few paragraphs of the content to give a clear idea of the topic at once.
4. **Distribution**: Distribute keywords evenly throughout the content. Use variants and synonyms to keep the text natural and interesting.
5. **Meta tags and URLs**: Ensure that keywords are present in meta titles, meta descriptions and URLs, as discussed above.

To recapitulate.

On-page optimization is a crucial element of SEO that requires attention to detail and a strategic approach. Creating quality content, using meta tags effectively, structuring URLs clearly, and integrating keywords naturally are all key steps to improve your website's ranking in search results. With a solid on-page optimization strategy, you can increase site visibility, attract relevant traffic, and achieve your digital marketing goals.

TECHNICAL OPTIMIZATION

Technical optimization is a key component of SEO that involves optimizing various aspects of a website's backend to improve its visibility and usability. This chapter will explore the importance of site speed, optimization for mobile devices, implementation of HTTPS, site structure and internal navigation, and the use of XML sitemaps and robots.txt files.

Importance of site speed

Site speed is important for user experience and search engine rankings. A slow site can lead to increased abandonment rates and reduced conversions. In addition, Google considers site speed a ranking factor. Here are some suggestions for improving site speed:

1. **Image optimization**: Reduce the size of images without compromising image quality. Use modern image formats such as WebP.
2. **Browser caching**: Implement caching to reduce page load times for returning visitors.
3. **Code reduction**: Minify CSS, JavaScript and HTML to reduce file size.
4. **Quality hosting**: Choose reliable and fast hosting to improve site performance.
5. **Content Delivery Network (CDN)**: Use a CDN to distribute content to servers close to visitors, reducing loading times.

Optimization for mobile devices

With the increased use of mobile devices for web browsing, it is essential that the site is optimized for these devices. Google uses mobile-first indexing, which means that the mobile version of the site is considered the primary version. Here's how to optimize for mobile devices:

1. **Responsive design**: Make sure the site automatically adapts to different screen sizes and resolutions.
2. **Loading speed on mobile:** Optimize site speed specifically for mobile devices.
3. **Mobile-Friendly Testing**: Use tools such as Google Mobile-Friendly Test to verify that the site is optimized for mobile devices.
4. **Intuitive navigation**: Ensure that navigation on mobile devices is simple and intuitive, with clear and easily accessible menus.

Implementation of HTTPS

HTTPS is the secure version of HTTP, which uses the SSL/TLS protocol to encrypt data between the browser and the server. Google considers HTTPS a ranking factor and displays a "not secure" warning for sites that do not use it. Here are the steps to implement HTTPS:

- **Purchase an SSL** certificate: Purchase an SSL certificate from a reputable provider.
- **Install the SSL certificate**: Install the certificate on the hosting server.

- **301 redirection**: Configure 301 redirects from HTTP versions of pages to HTTPS versions.
- **Update resources**: Ensure that all resources (images, scripts, CSS) are uploaded via HTTPS.
- **Security verification**: Use tools such as SSL Labs to verify that the site is completely secure.

Site structure and internal navigation

Good site structure and efficient internal navigation are essential for user experience and indexing by search engines. Here are some tips for optimizing site structure:

- **Hierarchical architecture**: Organize content in a hierarchical structure with clear categories and subcategories.
- **Navigation menu**: Create an intuitive navigation menu that allows users to easily find information.
- **Internal links**: Use internal links to connect related pages and improve content discovery by search engines.
- **Breadcrumbs**: Implement breadcrumbs to help users understand where they are within the site and facilitate navigation.

Using XML sitemap and robots.txt file

XML sitemaps and robots.txt files are essential tools for communicating with search engines and optimizing site indexing. Here's how to use them effectively:

1. **XML Sitemap**: Create an XML sitemap that lists all the important pages on the site. This helps search engines discover and index all relevant

pages. The sitemap can be generated using tools such as Yoast SEO or Screaming Frog.

2. **Sending the sitemap**: Send the XML sitemap to Google Search Console and other webmaster tools to make sure search engines use it.

3. **Robots.**txt file: Use the robots.txt file to control which parts of your site can be crawled by search engines. For example, you can block irrelevant folders or pages.

4. **Checking the robots.txt** file: Verify that the robots.txt file does not accidentally block important pages. Use tools such as Google Search Console's Robots.txt Tester.

To recapitulate.

Technical optimization is a crucial component of SEO that requires attention to the technical details of the website. Improving site speed, optimizing for mobile devices, implementing HTTPS, creating an effective site structure, and properly using XML sitemaps and robots.txt files are all critical steps to improve search engine rankings and provide a better user experience. With well-executed technical optimization, the site will be faster, safer and easier to navigate, leading to increased traffic and conversions.

Backlink Creation

Backlinks are one of the fundamental pillars of off-page SEO. A backlink is a link from another website pointing to yours. Search engines, particularly Google, view backlinks as a signal of trust and authority. In this chapter, we will explore what backlinks are and why they are important, strategies for getting quality backlinks, guest blogging and content outreach, and backlink analysis and monitoring.

What is a backlink and why is it important

A backlink is a hyperlink that comes from an external website and points to a page on your site. Backlinks are important for several reasons:

- **Site authority**: Search engines view backlinks as votes of confidence. The more quality backlinks you receive from authoritative sites, the higher the perception of your authority.
- **Search Engine Ranking**: Backlinks help improve ranking in SERPs (Search Engine Results Pages). Sites with many quality backlinks tend to rank better.
- **Referral Traffic**: Backlinks can generate direct traffic to your site. When a user clicks on a link pointing to your site, it becomes a referral visit.
- **Indexing**: Backlinks help search engines discover and index new pages. A site with many backlinks will be scanned more frequently by search engines.

Strategies for getting quality backlinks

Getting quality backlinks requires targeted strategies and continuous efforts. Here are some of the best practices for acquiring backlinks:

- **Creating valuable content**: High-quality content naturally attracts backlinks. Comprehensive guides, in-depth articles, infographics and original content tend to be shared and linked to more frequently.
- **Infographics**: Infographics are visually appealing and easy to share. Creating informative infographics and offering them to relevant blogs and sites can lead to valuable backlinks.
- **Link requests**: Contact relevant website owners and ask them to include a link to your content. It is important to personalize the request and explain the value your content can add to their readers.
- **Reviews and mentions**: Offering products or services in exchange for reviews can lead to backlinks. Also, monitor mentions of your brand online and ask that they be turned into active links.

Guest blogging and content outreach

Guest blogging and content outreach are two effective strategies for getting quality backlinks.

1. *Guest Blogging*: Writing articles for other blogs or sites in your industry can lead to backlinks and increase your visibility. Here are some steps for an effective guest blogging strategy:

- **Site identification**: Search for blogs and authoritative sites in your field that accept guest blogging articles.
- **Content proposal**: Contact site owners with proposals for content that is relevant and valuable to their audience.
- **Quality content creation**: Write high-quality articles that meet the needs of the host site's audience.
- **Link Inclusion**: Include backlinks to your site naturally within the content.

2. Content Outreach: Content outreach involves reaching out to bloggers, journalists and influencers to promote your content. Here's how to do it effectively:

- **Creating relevant content**: Create content that is of interest to your outreach recipients.
- **Contact identification**: Research and identify influential people and relevant sites that might be interested in your content.
- **Personalized emails**: Send personalized emails explaining why your content would be useful to them and their audience.
- **Follow-up**: Follow up with contacts who do not respond immediately to increase the chances of getting a link.

Backlink analysis and monitoring

Monitoring and analyzing backlinks is essential to understanding the effectiveness of your strategies and maintaining a healthy backlink profile. Here's how to do it:

1. **Monitoring Tools**: Use tools such as Ahrefs, SEMrush, Moz and Google Search Console to monitor your site's backlinks.
2. **Quality analysis**: Evaluate the quality of backlinks received. Backlinks from authoritative and relevant sites are more valuable.
3. **Identifying toxic links**: Detect and disavow low-quality or spam backlinks that could hurt your rankings.
4. **Competitor monitoring**: Analyze competitor backlinks to identify link-building opportunities and effective strategies.

To recapitulate.

Backlink building is a key component of off-page SEO. Backlinks not only improve search engine rankings, but also increase site authority and generate referral traffic. Using strategies such as quality content creation, guest blogging, content outreach, and ongoing monitoring, a strong and healthy backlink profile can be built. With a well-planned link-building strategy, your site will gain increased visibility, authority, and long-term success.

Using Social Media for SEO and Engagement

Social media is the latest born component of the digital marketing and SEO landscape, as it has only been around since the early 2000s. This article will explore the influence of social media on SEO, effective content sharing strategies, how to build an online community, and tracking engagement on social media.

The influence of social media on SEO

Although social media does not directly influence organic search engine rankings such as Google, it still plays a significant role in supporting SEO goals. Here are some ways in which social media can positively influence SEO:

1. **Increased content visibility**: Sharing high-quality content on social media can increase its visibility and lead to more website visits.

2. **Backlink generation**: Viralized content on social media can be linked from other sites, generating natural backlinks that improve site authority.

3. **Brand awareness and reputation**: A strong social media presence can increase brand recognition and trust, elements that can indirectly influence traffic and user behavior to the site.

4. **Indications of engagement**: Engagement on social media (likes, shares, comments) can be indicative of content quality and relevance, which are aspects

considered by Google and other search engines in determining rankings.

Strategies for sharing content on social media

To maximize the impact of social media on SEO, effective content sharing strategies are critical:

1. **Platform-friendly content**: Adapt content to the format and audience of each social platform (Facebook, Instagram, Twitter, LinkedIn, etc.).

2. **Frequency of publication**: Maintain a consistent frequency of publication, balancing between consistency and quality.

3. **Using hashtags**: Use relevant hashtags to expand the reach of content and reach new audiences.

4. **Audience Engagement**: Interact with the public through responses to comments, polls, contests, and other forms of engagement.

5. **Cross-promotion**: Promote content on different social channels to reach a wider audience.

Building an online community

Building a strong online community is an important and necessary step for long-term success on social media and beyond. Here are some steps for doing so:

1. **Identify your target audience**: Understand who your ideal followers are and what interests them.

2. **Create relevant content**: Offer content that addresses the needs and interests of your community.

3. **Fostering interaction**: Stimulating dialogue and sharing of experiences among community members.

4. Consistency **and authenticity**: Be consistent in tone and communication approach, maintaining an authentic and transparent image.

5. **Responding to feedback**: Taking into consideration the opinions and suggestions of the community to continuously improve.

Monitoring social media engagement

Monitoring social media engagement is essential to evaluate the effectiveness of your strategies and make any corrections. Here's how to do it:

1. **Engagement measures**: Monitor likes, shares, comments and other interactions with your content.

2. **Metrics analysis**: Use integrated or external analytical tools to measure engagement and derive useful insights.

3. **Identifying trends**: Detect the trends and content that attract the most interest in order to replicate or adapt them in the future.

4. **Conversion evaluation**: Link social media engagement to website conversions to understand the actual impact on SEO and business goals.

5. **Response and Adaptation**: Respond promptly to comments and interactions, adapting strategies according to the results obtained.

To recapitulate.

Social media is a powerful resource for improving online visibility, user engagement, and indirectly SEO ranking. By using targeted content sharing strategies, building a strong online community, and monitoring engagement effectively, the impact of social media on overall website performance can be maximized. Investing time and resources in social media management will not only help to improve online presence, but also to solidify brand reputation and achieve long-term business goals.

User Experience (UX) and SEO

User experience (UX) in SEO, directly influences user behavior and search engine rankings. This chapter will explore the importance of UX for SEO, intuitive design and easy navigation, optimization for loading speed, and the importance of continuous UX testing and improvements.

Importance of UX for SEO

UX refers to the overall quality of interaction users have with a website. A good user experience not only improves user engagement, but can also positively affect search engine rankings. This is how UX impacts SEO:

1. **Low bounce rate**: A site with a positive user experience tends to have a lower bounce rate, which indicates to search engine algorithms that the content is relevant and meets user expectations.

2. **Dwell time**: An optimized UX can increase the time users spend on the site, another positive signal to search engines that indicates the content is interesting and useful.

3. **Ease of navigation**: An intuitive navigation structure makes it easy for users to find what they are looking for, improving the experience and reducing the abandonment rate.

4. **Positive feedback**: Satisfied users tend to share the content and create links, indirectly contributing to off-page SEO.

Intuitive design and easy navigation

Intuitive design and easy navigation are pillars of effective UX. Here are some principles for improving UX through design and navigation:

1. **Clarity and consistency**: Maintain a consistent layout throughout the site, with a clean, easy-to-navigate design.

2. **Navigation structure**: Use clear and intuitive menus that guide users through the site without confusion.

3. **Mobile Usability**: Ensure that the site is fully responsive and provides an optimal user experience on all devices, including smartphones and tablets.

4. **Minimize clicks**: Reduce the number of clicks required to reach the desired information, simplifying the user's journey.

5. **Effective Call-to-Action (CTA)**: Use well-placed and clearly visible CTAs to guide users to desired actions (e.g., purchases, sign-ups, contacts).

Optimization for loading speed

Site loading speed is another crucial aspect of UX that directly affects SEO. Here is why it is important:

1. **Impact on user experience**: Fast sites provide a better user experience, reducing wait time and improving overall satisfaction.

2. **Ranking factor**: Google considers site speed as a ranking factor. Fast sites tend to rank better in search results.

3. **Conversion rates**: A slow site can increase abandonment rates and reduce conversions. Improving speed can lead to better results in terms of conversions.

Continuous testing and improvement of the UX

Continuous improvement of the UX is essential to adapt to the changing needs of users and to maximize the potential of the website. Here is how to carry out UX testing and improvement:

1. **Data analysis**: Use analytical tools such as Google Analytics to monitor user behavior and identify areas for improvement.

2. **A/B** testing: Conduct A/B tests to compare different versions of pages and determine which offers a better user experience.

3. **User feedback**: Collect direct feedback from users through surveys, interviews, or analysis of behavior on the site.

4. **Data-driven optimization**: Use collected data to make incremental improvements, such as changes to design, navigation, or content.

5. **Constant** monitoring: Continue to monitor UX metrics and make regular adjustments to ensure an optimal user experience over time.

Conclusion

User experience is a key element for SEO success. A website with a well-designed UX not only improves search engine rankings, but also increases user engagement, conversions, and brand reputation. Investing in creating an intuitive design, easy navigation, optimized loading speed, and continuous UX improvements is essential to maintaining a competitive advantage online. With a well-planned UX strategy, the site not only attracts more visitors, but also converts them into loyal and satisfied customers.

Local SEO: the last frontier of SEO

Local SEO is critical for businesses that want to attract local customers through search engines. This chapter will explore what it means to do local SEO, the importance of optimizing on Google My Business, collecting and managing reviews, and effective strategies for local businesses.

Understanding local SEO

Local SEO focuses on optimizing the website for geographically relevant search results. It is especially important for companies with a physical presence or that offer services in a specific geographic area. The main goals of local SEO include:

- **Increase local visibility**: Appear in the top positions in search results when users search for local products or services.

- **Attract local customers**: Drive web traffic to the website from users who are physically close to the business.

- **Increase offline sales**: Facilitate the conversion of web traffic into sales or physical visits to the business.

Google My Business Optimization

Google My Business (GMB) is a crucial tool for local SEO optimization. Here's how to use it effectively:

1. **Create and update profile**: Make sure all information about the business is complete and accurate, including address, phone number, business hours, and business categories.

2. **Review management**: Monitor and respond to customer reviews in a timely manner, both positive and negative, to improve the company's online reputation.

3. **Inclusion of photos and videos**: Upload high-quality images and videos showing the inside and outside of the company, the products offered, and the team.

4. **Posting**: Use the Google My Business post feature to share updates, promotions and events with local audiences.

5. **Performance Analysis**: Monitor Google My Business analytics to understand how users interact with the profile and make data-driven improvements.

Collection and management of reviews

Customer reviews play a crucial role in local SEO and company reputation. Here's how to manage them effectively:

1. **Incentivize reviews**: Ask satisfied customers to leave a review on Google, Yelp or other relevant platforms.

2. **Respond to reviews**: Show appreciation for positive reviews and respond promptly to negative reviews to resolve any problems.

3. **Monitor reviews**: Use review monitoring tools to be notified whenever a new review is posted.

4. **Use feedback for improvements**: Use feedback from customers to improve products, services and the overall customer experience.

Strategies for local activities

Strategies for local business aim to improve the company's visibility and attractiveness in its local community. Here are some effective approaches:

1. **Local on-page SEO**: Include the name of the city or region in page titles, meta descriptions, and content to indicate geographic relevance.

2. **Local content creation**: Write content that is relevant to the local community, such as articles about local events, community news, or local success stories.

3. **Local backlinks**: Get backlinks from local authoritative sites, such as local chambers of commerce, industry associations, or local blogs.

4. **Community involvement**: Actively participate in local events, sponsor local organizations and collaborate with other local businesses to increase visibility.

5. **Mobile and location**: Make sure the website is fully optimized for mobile devices, as many local users search for information on smartphones or tablets.

Conclusion

Local SEO is essential for businesses that want to tap into the local market and attract relevant customers through search engines. Optimizing Google My Business, managing customer reviews, implementing local strategies, and constantly improving local visibility are all key tactics for success in local SEO. Investing in local SEO not only improves online visibility, but can also increase qualified traffic, conversions, and long-term growth for the business in its area of operation.

Monitoring and Analysis for Effective SEO

Monitoring and analysis are critical to assessing the effectiveness of SEO strategies and making ongoing improvements. This chapter will explore the importance of SEO analysis tools, monitoring traffic and site performance, keyword and content analysis, and using Google Analytics and Google Search Console to optimize online presence.

SEO analysis tools

Using the right SEO analysis tools is essential to understanding how your website ranks in search engines and identifying opportunities for improvement. Here are some key tools:

1. **Google Analytics**: Provides detailed data on site traffic, user engagement, traffic sources and conversions. It is critical for monitoring overall site performance and identifying strengths and weaknesses.

2. **Google Search Console**: Provides information about the site's search performance, such as page indexing, search queries for which the site appears, security issues, and more. It is useful for monitoring the appearance and ranking of the site in search results.

3. **Ahrefs**: Comprehensive tool for backlink analysis, keyword analysis, competitive analysis and more. Useful for identifying effective link building strategies and monitoring keyword position.

4. **Moz Pro**: Offers domain authority metrics, keyword analysis, backlink tracking and more. Helps monitor and improve organic ranking.

5. **SEMrush**: All-in-one tool for keyword research, competitive analysis, SEO audit, online advertising and more. It is ideal for getting a comprehensive overview of SEO performance.

Monitoring traffic and site performance

Monitoring website traffic and performance provides valuable insights to improve user experience and optimize conversions. Here's what to monitor:

1. **Visits and unique users**: Monitor the number of visits to the site and the number of unique users to understand overall traffic trends.

2. **Dwell time**: Measure how long users spend on the site to assess engagement and interest in content.

3. **Bounce** rate: Check the bounce rate to see how many people leave the site after visiting a single page. A high bounce rate may indicate usability or content problems.

4. **Conversions**: Track conversions, which can be purchases, sign-ups, downloads, or other desired actions, to evaluate the effectiveness of call-to-actions and landing pages.

5. **Most visited pages**: Identify the most visited pages to understand what topics or products users are most interested in.

Keyword and content analysis

Keyword and content analysis is crucial for optimizing search engine rankings and attracting relevant traffic. Here's how to do it:

1. **Keyword research**: Use tools such as Google Keyword Planner, Ahrefs, SEMrush or others to identify keywords relevant to your industry and geographic location.

2. **Monitoring keyword positions**: Keep track of keyword positions to monitor progress and identify opportunities for improvement.

3. **Content audit**: Regularly assess the quality and relevance of content. Update existing content to maintain relevance and create new content to cover emerging topics.

4. **Competition**: Analyze competitors' content strategies to identify untapped opportunities and improve your own strategies.

Using Google Analytics and Google Search Console

Google Analytics and Google Search Console are free tools provided by Google and are essential for monitoring and improving SEO performance. Here's how to use them effectively:

1. **Google Analytics**:
   - Monitor key metrics such as traffic, conversions, user behavior and more.
   - Identify input pages, output pages, and user navigation paths to optimize user experience.
   - Use segments to analyze specific user groups and behaviors.
2. **Google Search Console**:
   - Verify site ownership and monitor page indexing by Google.
   - Analyze the search queries for which the site appeared, the impressions and the CTR (Click-Through Rate).
   - Identify and resolve any indexing or security problems.

To recapitulate.

Monitoring and analytics are critical to SEO success. By using the right tools such as Google Analytics, Google Search Console and other SEO analytics platforms, you can gain detailed insights into website performance, keyword trends and user engagement. This data allows you to identify optimization opportunities, improve search engine rankings, and provide a superior user experience. Investing in ongoing monitoring and analysis is essential to maintaining a competitive advantage and achieving long-term business goals through SEO.

SEO for E-commerce

SEO for e-commerce sites is critical for increasing online visibility, attracting qualified traffic, and increasing sales. This chapter will explore the specifics of SEO for e-commerce sites, product sheet optimization, SEO for product categories, and effective strategies to increase conversion rates.

Specificity of SEO for e-commerce sites

SEO for e-commerce websites presents unique challenges compared to other types of websites. Key considerations include:

- **Wide range of products**: Managing a large number of product pages and categories requires careful organization and optimization.

- **Dynamic content**: Products can be added, changed or removed frequently, making automation and efficiency in SEO processes crucial.

- **Online competition**: The e-commerce industry is highly competitive, with numerous competitors trying to rank for the same keywords and product categories.

- **Conversion needs**: In addition to organic traffic, it is crucial to optimize the site to maximize conversions, such as through user experience and call-to-action optimization.

Optimization of product sheets

Product sheets are the backbone of an e-commerce site and must be optimized to attract traffic and convert visitors into customers. Here's how to do it:

1. **Detailed descriptions**: Write unique, detailed and relevant descriptions that include relevant keywords and useful information for potential buyers.

2. **High-quality images**: Use high-quality product images showing the product from different angles and in use situations if possible.

3. **Keywords**: Include relevant keywords in product title, descriptions and image alt tags to improve search engine rankings.

4. **Customer reviews**: Customer reviews not only improve product credibility but can also improve SEO ranking through user-generated content.

5. **URL structure**: Use optimized URLs that include the product name and category to improve understandability and ranking.

SEO for product categories

Product category pages are critical for organizing and presenting products clearly and in a way that is accessible to search engines. Here's how to optimize them:

1. **Hierarchical** structure: Use a logical and clear hierarchical structure for categories, subcategories and products.

2. **Unique content**: Ensure that each category has a unique and relevant description that includes relevant keywords.

3. **Intuitive** navigation: Create a smooth navigation experience with clear menus and search filters that allow users to easily find what they are looking for.

4. **Cross-linking**: Use internal links to link product category pages to each other and to related products to improve user experience and indexing.

5. **Image optimization**: Optimize product category images with descriptive and relevant alt tags.

Strategies to increase conversion rate

In addition to SEO, it is crucial to implement strategies to increase the conversion rate on e-commerce sites. Here are some effective strategies:

1. **Reviews and testimonials**: Use customer reviews and testimonials to increase buyer confidence and influence purchasing decisions.

2. **Clear Call-to-Action (CTA)**: Use clear, well-placed CTAs to guide users to purchase or other desired actions.

3. **Offers and promotions**: Use special offers, discounts and promotions to incentivize purchases and increase a sense of urgency.

4. **Streamlined user experience**: Ensure that the purchasing process is simple and intuitive, with

only a few steps between product selection and order completion.

5. **Visual testimonials**: Use videos, pictures and other visual content showing products in action to enhance interest and understanding.

To recapitulate.

SEO for e-commerce is essential for increasing visibility, traffic and online sales. Optimizing product sheets, product categories, and implementing strategies to improve conversion rates are all key steps to success. Investing in SEO for e-commerce not only improves search engine rankings but also increases consumer attractiveness and trust, thereby improving overall e-commerce performance. By following best practices and constantly monitoring performance, companies can successfully position themselves in the competitive e-commerce market.

Multimedia Content: Enhancing SEO with Images, Videos and Infographics

Multimedia content plays a crucial role in modern SEO, enhancing the user experience and increasing engagement on the website. This chapter will explore image optimization, the use of video for SEO, the implementation of infographics, and the overall impact of multimedia content on SEO.

Image optimization

Images not only make content more visually appealing but can also improve SEO if optimized properly. Here are some key practices:

- **Size and compression**: Upload images with web-optimized sizes and compress them to reduce page load times.

- **Alternative text (ALT)**: Use descriptive ALT tags that include relevant keywords to help search engines understand what the image is about.

- **File name**: Name image files meaningfully, using keywords when appropriate (e.g., "shoes-running-nike.jpg" instead of "img123.jpg").

- **Appropriate format**: Use web-friendly image formats such as JPEG for photographs and PNG for images with transparent backgrounds.

Using video for SEO

Videos are one of the most powerful content to engage users and improve SEO. Here's how to integrate them effectively:

1. **Optimized video creation**: Produce high-quality videos that are relevant to the theme of the website and include keywords in the title, description and tags.

2. **Embedding and hosting**: Uploading videos to popular platforms such as YouTube and embedding them on website pages. This not only improves the user experience but can also increase visibility in Google video searches.

3. **Subtitles and transcripts**: Add subtitles and provide a text transcript of the video to improve accessibility and help search engines understand the content of the video.

4. **Video SEO**: Optimize video pages with descriptive titles, detailed descriptions, relevant tags and eye-catching thumbnails to maximize visibility.

5. **Promotion and sharing**: Promote videos through social media, email marketing and other platforms to increase views and engagement.

Implementation of infographics

Infographics combine visual and textual information to communicate complex concepts clearly and attractively. Here's how they can improve SEO:

1. **Clear and appealing design**: Create visually appealing infographics that are easy to understand and share.

2. **Information content**: Provide useful and relevant information that is relevant to the target audience.

3. **SEO optimization**: Use relevant keywords in the title, description and metadata of the infographic to improve search engine rankings.

4. **Embedding and sharing**: Enable users to easily embed infographics on their websites or blogs, thereby increasing visibility and traffic.

5. **Promotion**: Promote infographics through social media, email marketing and other channels to increase their reach and engagement.

Impact of multimedia content on SEO

Multimedia content not only enhances the user experience but also has a direct impact on SEO. Here's how:

1. **Improved engagement**: Visual and interactive content such as images, videos, and infographics increase user engagement, reducing bounce rates and increasing time spent on the site.

2. **Increased sharing and backlinks**: High-quality multimedia content is more likely to be shared on social media and websites, generating natural backlinks that improve site authority.

3. **Improved user experience**: A website that offers well-integrated multimedia content creates a

positive user experience, which in turn can improve search engine rankings.

4. **Content diversification**: Using various types of content (textual, visual, audio) helps meet the consumption preferences of different users, increasing the overall reach of SEO.

5. **Abandonment rate reduction**: High-quality multimedia content can reduce site abandonment rate, thereby improving SEO metrics such as dwell time and bounce rate.Conclusion

To recapitulate

Strategic use of images, videos, and infographics can transform a website's SEO, significantly improving user engagement, online visibility, and site authority. Optimizing this content for relevant keywords, integrating it into the overall SEO strategy, and monitoring performance metrics are crucial steps to exploit the full potential of multimedia content. Investing in the creation and optimization of high-quality multimedia content not only improves SEO but also the user experience, leading to long-term benefits for the website's online success.

SEO and Content Marketing: A Winning Synergy

The synergy between SEO and content marketing is a key pillar of any company's online success. This chapter will explore how to effectively integrate these two disciplines, plan an effective content strategy, create evergreen content, and promote it to maximize SEO impact.

Synergy between SEO and content marketing

SEO and content marketing are closely interconnected and support each other to achieve common goals:

- **SEO as a strategic guide**: SEO provides precise guidance on what users are looking for and how to optimize content to meet these needs.

- **Content marketing for value creation**: Content marketing focuses on creating relevant, useful and high-quality content that responds to users' questions and needs.

- **Keyword integration**: Strategic integration of keywords in content creation improves search engine rankings, thereby increasing organic visibility.

Planning a content strategy

Detailed planning is essential to the success of SEO-oriented content marketing:

1. **Target Audience Analysis**: Understand who your ideal customers are, what their problems are, and how your content can help them.

2. **Keyword research**: Identify keywords relevant to your industry and use them to guide content creation.

3. **Clear goals**: Define specific goals for each piece of content, which may include improving SEO ranking, increasing organic traffic or increasing conversions.

4. **Editorial calendar**: Create an editorial calendar to plan content publication based on seasonal events, market trends and marketing goals.

Evergreen content creation

Evergreen content is that content that maintains its relevance over time and continues to generate organic traffic over the long term:

1. **Focus on evergreen topics**: Choose topics and subjects that do not quickly become obsolete, such as detailed guides, step-by-step tutorials and educational resources.

2. **In-depth and comprehensive**: Offer in-depth and comprehensive content that fully answers users' questions and outperforms the competition.

3. **Periodic** updates: Keep evergreen content updated with fresh and relevant information to continue to provide value to users and maintain SEO ranking.

Content distribution and promotion

Effective promotion of content is essential to maximize its impact and visibility:

1. **Social media**: Share content through social channels to reach a wider audience and generate natural backlinks.

2. **Email marketing**: Use email marketing to promote new content to subscribers and keep them informed of the latest resources.

3. **Collaborations and influencers**: Collaborate with influencers in the field to expand content reach and increase authority.

4. **On-page SEO**: Optimize content with META tags, SEO-friendly URL structure and strategic keywords to improve search engine rankings.

To recapitulate.

Effective integration of SEO and content marketing not only improves search engine rankings but also increases user engagement and conversions. Planning a content strategy based on keyword research, creating high-quality evergreen content, and promoting it through diverse channels are critical to long-term success. Investing in SEO-oriented content marketing not only increases online visibility but also establishes brand authority and trustworthiness in your industry. With a well-defined strategy and diligent implementation, companies can successfully meet and exceed their online marketing goals.

Essential SEO Tools: Boost Your Strategy with the Right Resources

Using SEO tools is critical for monitoring, analyzing, and optimizing your website's performance in search engines. This chapter will explore an overview of the best SEO tools available, their practical use to improve your digital strategy, and how they can help with keyword and backlink analysis.

Overview of the best SEO tools

There are numerous SEO tools available, each with unique features to meet different needs. Here are some of the most widely used and valued in the industry:

1. **Google Analytics**: Free tool to monitor web traffic, traffic sources and user behavior on the site.

2. **Google Search Console**: Provides data on website visibility in Google search results, suggestions for fixing technical problems, and performance analysis.

3. **Ahrefs**: Used for backlink analysis, keyword research, search engine ranking monitoring, and competitive analysis.

4. **SEMrush**: Provides detailed data on keywords, organic traffic, backlinks, SEO audits and competitive analysis.

5. **Moz Pro**: Includes tools for keyword research, SEO audit, ranking monitoring and backlink analysis.

6. **SEOptimer**: Offers comprehensive SEO audit, keyword monitoring, site performance reports, and competitive analysis.

7. **SpyFu**: Tool for competitive analysis, keyword research, and SEO and PPC performance monitoring.

Practical use of tools

SEO tools can be used in various ways to optimize your website and improve SEO performance:

1. **Keyword Analysis**: Use tools such as Ahrefs, SEMrush or Google Keyword Planner to identify keywords relevant to your industry, assess search volume and competitive intensity.

2. **Ranking monitoring**: Track your website's positions for target keywords and monitor fluctuations in search results using tools such as SEMrush, Moz Pro or SEOptimer.

3. **Backlink analysis**: Use tools such as Ahrefs or Moz Pro to analyze incoming backlinks, assess backlink quality, and identify opportunities to acquire new quality backlinks.

4. **SEO audits**: Perform regular SEO audits to identify technical problems, such as crawl errors, URL structure issues, or site speed issues, using tools such as SEOptimer or SEMrush.

Tools for analysis and monitoring

- **Google Analytics**: Monitors web traffic, user engagement and conversions.

- **Google Search Console**: Provides detailed search performance data, optimization suggestions, and technical troubleshooting.

- **Ahrefs**: Analyze website backlinks, monitor keyword rankings and organic traffic trends.

- **SEMrush**: Offers detailed keyword reports, competitive analysis, SEO audits and ranking monitoring.

Tools for keyword research and backlinks

- **Ahrefs**: Keyword research, backlink analysis, position monitoring and detailed competitive reports.

- **SEMrush**: Keyword analysis, position monitoring, SEO audit and competitive keyword research.

- **Moz Pro**: Keyword research, position tracking, backlink analysis and SEO audit.

- **Google Keyword Planner**: Free Google tool for finding and analyzing keywords for advertising campaigns.

To recapitulate

SEO tools are essential for improving your website's visibility, traffic, and overall search engine performance. By using the right tools, you can gain valuable data, identify opportunities for improvement, and constantly monitor your SEO strategies. Investing in effective SEO tools not only optimizes your time and resources but also increases your chances of success in today's competitive digital landscape. Make the most of the potential of SEO tools to rank high in search results and maintain a competitive advantage over the long term.

Conclusions and Future Perspectives in SEO

SEO is an ever-evolving field that is crucial to the online success of any business. This chapter will summarize the key concepts covered in our journey through the different aspects of SEO, explore the future prospects of this discipline, and provide tips on how to stay current in the dynamic world of SEO.

Summary of key concepts

During our journey through the various chapters, we explored:

- **What is SEO**: SEO is the set of practices designed to improve a website's visibility in organic search results.

- **Importance of SEO in digital marketing**: SEO is crucial for attracting qualified traffic, improving user experience and increasing conversions.

- **Evolving Google algorithms**: Google regularly updates its algorithms to improve the relevance of search results and user experience.

- **Realistic goals and expectations**: It is important to set clear goals, monitor performance, and continually adjust strategies to achieve sustainable results over time.

- **Advanced SEO Strategies**: From keyword research to technical optimization, from backlink creation to social media management, every aspect contributes to the overall success of SEO.

Future perspectives of SEO

The future of SEO is set to evolve further, with some key trends that we can anticipate:

- **Artificial intelligence and machine learning**: Google will continue to integrate technologies such as BERT to improve natural language understanding and provide more relevant search results.

- **Semantic and voice search: As** the use of voice assistants such as Siri and Alexa increases, semantic and voice search will become increasingly relevant, requiring content optimization based on more conversational queries.

- **Mobile SEO**: With an increasing number of users accessing content via mobile devices, mobile optimization will continue to be a priority to improve user experience and search engine rankings.

- **Media content**: Images, videos and infographics will continue to play a crucial role in user engagement and SEO optimization.

How to stay current in the world of SEO

To stay abreast of rapid developments in the field of SEO, it is essential to adopt these practices:

1. **Continuing Education**: Attend webinars, conferences, and trainings to stay up-to-date on the latest SEO trends and best practices.

2. **Follow industry experts**: Keep informed by reading blogs, following influencers and participating in discussions in industry forums.

3. **Use monitoring tools**: Use advanced SEO tools such as Google Analytics, Google Search Console, Ahrefs, SEMrush, Moz and others to monitor your site's performance and identify opportunities for improvement.

4. **Experiment and adapt**: Test new strategies and techniques to see what works best for your website and continually adapt your strategy based on the results you get.

5. Networking: Participate in online and offline networking groups to share knowledge, experiences and strategies with other professionals in the field.

Conclusion

SEO is a vital element for success in digital marketing, and its importance will continue to grow in the future.

Being well prepared, informed and agile are the keys to adapting to rapid changes in Google's algorithms and new trends in user behavior. Investing in SEO is not only an investment in ranking your site in search engines but also in creating a superior user experience and achieving your business goals. With a well-defined strategy and a continuous search for improvements, you can position yourself to best meet the challenges and take advantage of opportunities in the competitive online world of today and tomorrow.

APPENDIX

Glossary of SEO terms

Here is a glossary of essential SEO terms that can help you better understand the world of Search Engine Optimization:

1. **SEO (Search Engine Optimization)**: Search engine optimization; set of techniques to improve a website's visibility in organic search results.

2. **SERP (Search Engine** Results Page): Page of search results shown by a search engine after a user enters a query.

3. **Keyword (Keyword)**: Specific word or phrase used by users in search engines to find information related to a particular topic.

4. **Long-tail keyword**: Longer, more specific search phrase that is less competitive than more generic keywords.

5. **Backlink**: Hyperlink from another website to your site. Backlinks are important for improving authority and SEO ranking.

6. **Link building**: Activities of obtaining backlinks from other websites to improve authority and SEO ranking.

7. **Meta tags**: HTML tags that provide information about the content of a web page to search engines.

The most common are the meta title and meta description.

8. **Meta title**: Title of a web page displayed in search results as the main title.

9. **Meta description**: Brief description of a web page that appears below the title in search results.

10.   **Crawler (or Spider)**: A program used by search engines to explore and index web pages available on the Internet.

11.   **Indexing (Indexing)**: Process in which search engines store and organize web pages in a database to provide relevant search results.

12.   **PageRank**: Algorithm developed by Google to assess the relevance and authority of a web page based on incoming links.

13.   **Anchor** text: Clickable text of a hyperlink. Anchor text is important for correctly indexing the content of the landing page.

14.   **Alt** text: Alternative text associated with an image used by search engines to understand the content of the image, particularly for accessibility.

15.   **Canonical tag**: HTML tag used to indicate the preferred version of a web page when there is duplicate or similar content.

16.   **Black Hat** SEO: Unethical SEO practices that are contrary to search engine guidelines and aimed at fraudulently manipulating search results.

17. **White Hat SEO**: Ethical SEO practices that comply with search engine guidelines to improve a website's visibility.

18. **Grey Hat SEO**: SEO practices that may be considered ethical but potentially risky or ambiguous according to search engine guidelines.

19. **Impressions (Impressions)**: Number of times a web page was displayed in search results, regardless of whether it was clicked on or not.

20. **CTR (Click-Through Rate)**: Percentage of users who click on a link compared to the number of times the link was viewed (impressions).

Resources and recommended readings

Here are some recommended resources and readings to learn more about SEO and stay up-to-date on best practices and strategies:

Books

1. **"The Art of SEO"** by Eric Enge, Stephan Spencer, Jessie Stricchiola, Rand Fishkin: A comprehensive book covering all aspects of SEO, from technical optimization to content strategy and link building.

2. **"SEO 2024: Learn Search Engine Optimization with Smart Internet Marketing Strategies"** by Adam Clarke: An updated guide that explores the latest SEO and digital marketing strategies for improving search engine rankings.

3. **"SEO for Growth: The Ultimate Guide for Marketers, Web Designers & Entrepreneurs"** by John Jantsch and Phil Singleton: A book that connects SEO to broader marketing strategies, offering an integrated approach to achieving tangible results.

Websites and Blogs

1. **Moz Blog**: One of the most authoritative resources in the field of SEO, offering articles, guides and resources for all levels of expertise.

2. **Search Engine Land**: A website dedicated to the latest news, strategies and updates in the world of search engines and SEO.

3. **Backlinko**: Created by Brian Dean, Backlinko is known for its in-depth guides and advanced tactics for link building and content optimization.

4. **SEMrush Blog**: Offers in-depth articles and research on SEO, PPC, social media and digital marketing in general.

Practical Tools and Resources

1. **Google Analytics Academy**: Free courses offered by Google to learn how to use Google Analytics to monitor and analyze web traffic.

2. **Google Search Console Help**: Official Google resources for understanding how to best use Google Search Console to optimize your site for search.

These resources will help you gain a thorough understanding of SEO and implement effective strategies to improve your website's search engine rankings. Remember to keep exploring and updating regularly, as the field of SEO is constantly evolving with new techniques and algorithms to consider.

Complete SEO checklist

Here is a comprehensive SEO checklist to optimize a website and improve its visibility in search engines:

SEO Checklist for On-Page Optimization

Keyword Search

- ☑ Identifies relevant keywords for each page of the site.
- ☑ Use tools such as Google Keyword Planner, Ahrefs, SEMrush for keyword research.
- ☑ Choose long-tail (long-tail) keywords that are relevant to the content of the page.
- ☑ Considers users' search intent for each selected keyword.

Content Optimization

- ☑ Create high-quality content that is original and relevant to the theme of the page.
- ☑ Use keywords naturally in the title, subtitles, and body of the text.
- ☑ Make sure the content is well structured with short paragraphs, bulleted lists, and clear subtitles.
- ☑ Incorporate multimedia content such as optimized images, videos, and infographics to improve user engagement.
- ☑ Write persuasive and descriptive meta tags for the meta title and meta description.

Technical Optimization

- ☑ Make sure the site is accessible to users and search engines. Avoid the use of black hat SEO techniques.
- ☑ Optimize page loading speed using tools such as Google PageSpeed Insights.
- ☑ Implements the HTTPS protocol to ensure a secure connection.
- ☑ Verify that the site is mobile-friendly and optimized for mobile devices.
- ☑ Use a simple and readable URL structure, with keywords when possible.

Site Structure and Internal Navigation

- ☑ Create an intuitive and easy-to-follow navigation structure for users.
- ☑ Use breadcrumbs to indicate the location of the page on the site.
- ☑ Create a robots.txt file to tell search engines which pages should be indexed.
- ☑ Uses an XML sitemap to facilitate indexing of pages by search engines.

SEO Checklist for Off-Page Optimization

Link Building

- ☑ Acquire backlinks from authoritative websites relevant to your industry.
- ☑ Use guest blogging techniques to get backlinks from influential sites.

- ☑ Actively participate in relevant communities and forums, contributing valuable links.

Social Media and Engagement

- ☑ Promote website content through social media to increase visibility and traffic.
- ☑ Create a content sharing strategy to engage your audience and build an online community.
- ☑ Monitor engagement on social media to understand what works best with your audience.

Checklist for Analysis and Monitoring

SEO Analysis Tools

- ☑ Uses Google Analytics to monitor web traffic, traffic sources, and user behavior.
- ☑ Employs Google Search Console to analyze search performance, identify technical problems, and improve indexing.
- ☑ Use tools such as Ahrefs, SEMrush or Moz to monitor keyword rankings and backlink analysis.

Performance Monitoring

- ☑ Regularly monitor website performance to identify any problems and opportunities for optimization.
- ☑ Conduct periodic SEO audits to ensure that the site complies with current best practices and standards.

Checklist for Local SEO

Local Optimization

- ☑ Create and optimize profile on Google My Business to improve local visibility.
- ☑ Manage and respond to customer reviews to build reputation and trust.

To sum up.

By following this SEO checklist, you can significantly improve your website's visibility in search engines, attract qualified traffic, and improve user experience. Remember that SEO is an ongoing process of monitoring, analyzing and optimizing to adapt to algorithm updates and the changing needs of users and search engines.